Chinese Modern New Technology Series

Artificial Intelligence

Edited by Li Chaodong

Translated by Xuemeng Angela Li

河海大學出版社
HOHAI UNIVERSITY PRESS

ROYAL COLLINS
Books Beyond Boundaries

46.98%
WIN

“Dad, what is **Artificial Intelligence**?” Dongdong asks.

“Here is an example. In 2016, the Korean professional 9-dan Go player Lee Sedol was beaten by AlphaGo. Machines that can think and strategize like AlphaGo is what we call artificial intelligence, which was shortened to AI,” Dad replies.

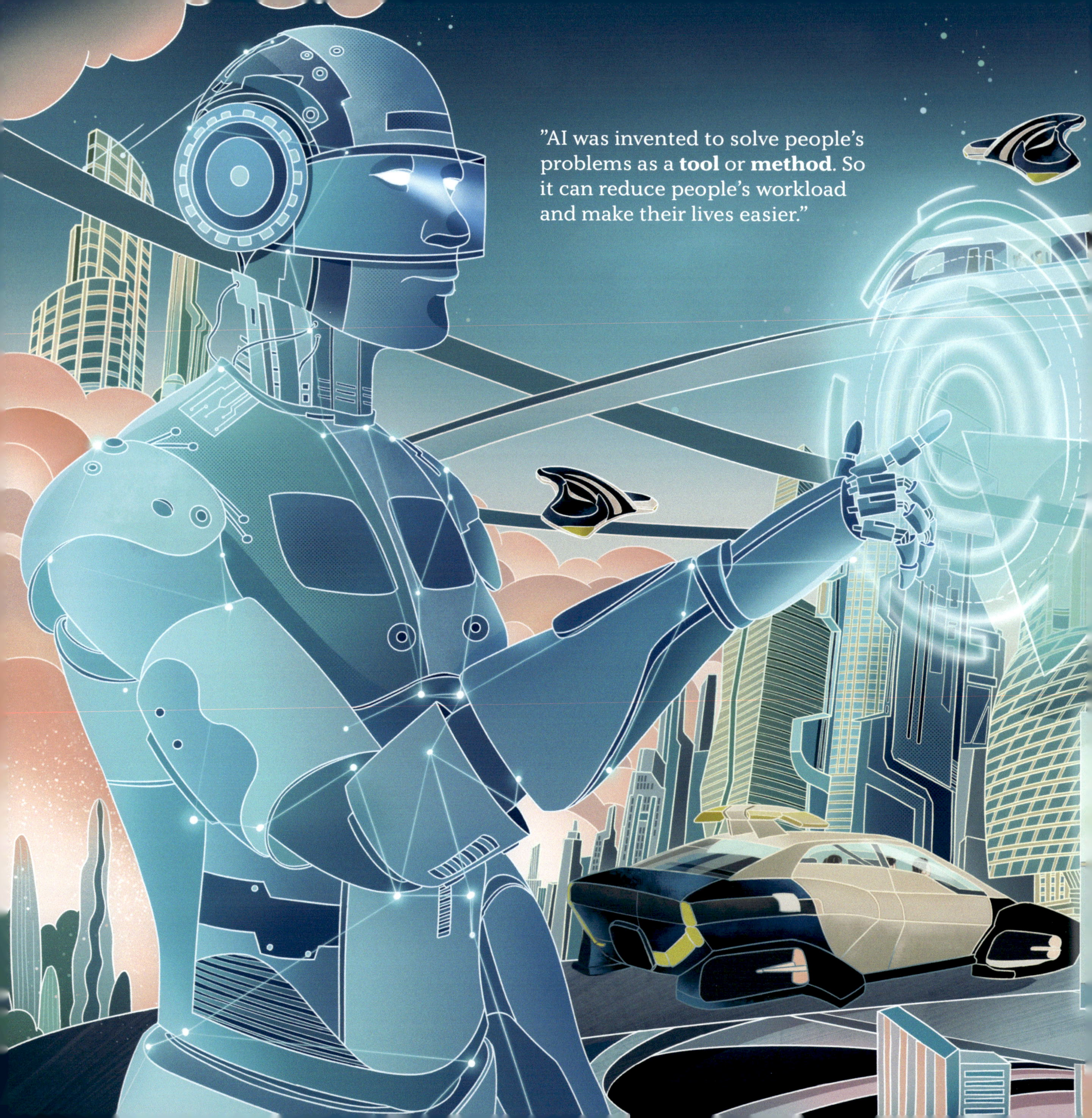

"AI was invented to solve people's problems as a **tool** or **method**. So it can reduce people's workload and make their lives easier."

Summary
Observation
Execution

"Why AI can make decisions?" Dongdong becomes really curious.
"To answer your question, we need to explain the three pillars of AI: **Computing Power**, **Algorithms**, and **Big Data**."
Computing Power
From record-keeping knots to manual calculation, the computing speed has significantly accelerated. But it still wasn't fast enough, so people invented the abacus. The functions of abacus are incredibly powerful, through which the first atomic bomb of China was developed.

Later, computers with higher competency were created. **Supercomputers** operate even faster, and the "Shenwei TaihuLight" model computes two million times faster than regular home computers.

Just like many solutions can be available to one problem, AI works with various **algorithms**. The most mainstream algorithm is **machine learning**, which allows machines to observe, conclude, and learn like infants. Algorithms can accelerate the computing speed of computers. For example, if you'd like to find all the books in your library that have "AI" in their titles, it might take several months through a manual search. But the algorithm can complete that task within seconds.

Neural network is currently the most popular algorithm. It is inspired by **human brains** and enables computers to think in steps and develop a thinking model with a network structure just like human brains.

AI can now operate at full capacity with developed algorithms, devices, and tremendous data available.

Since not all the data collected are useful, it requires us to analyze and label the data first.

The Internet has enabled the transparency of all user data. It can get to know the "real you" without meeting you. We can now analyze one person's data and find out information such as age, sex, occupation, income, location, educational level, shopping habits, family background, and hobbies. Data can support subsequent corporate decision-making by classifying and **developing profiles** for similar target audiences and matching them with appropriate product features.

"That's amazing! Dad, are there any other AI applications around us?" Dongdong asks with curiosity.

"Although AI is less than 100 years old, it has penetrated all aspects of our lives."

In locations such as airports, train stations, residential blocks, and office buildings, people can complete their identity verification through **facial recognition** and also expedite registration. AI also simplifies police work by summarizing and analyzing the behaviors and traces of suspects, comparing their facial information, and quickly locating them, which assists police with the arrest procedure.

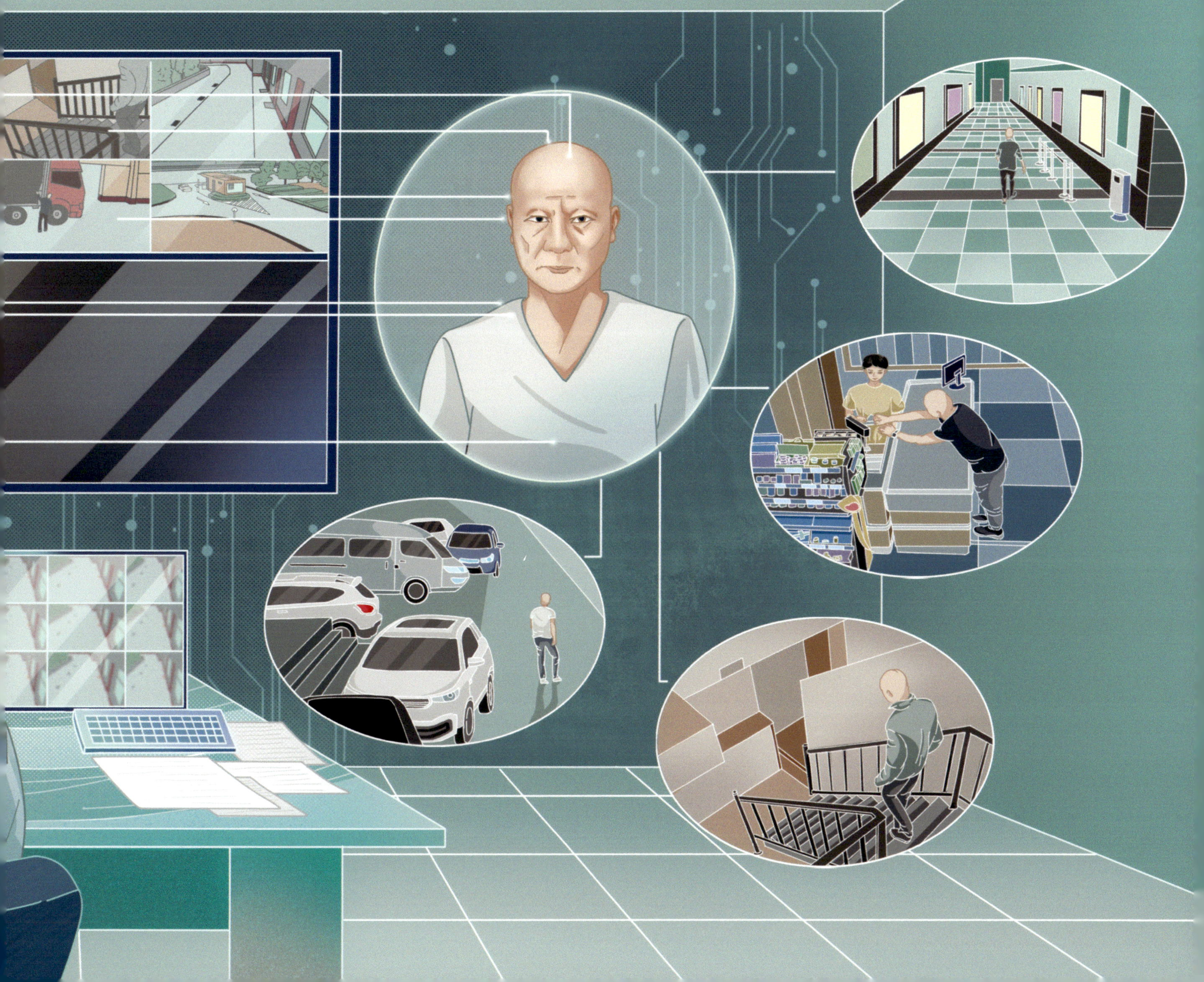

If you feel sick, you can also consult **virtual assistants**, who will provide analysis and diagnosis based on the described symptoms.

It can also read your medical records and examination results to help doctors understand your situation better.

AI can even be used in the **pharmaceutical industry and surgery procedures**. It does not actually research and develop the medicines. Instead, it simulates the manufacturing process in computers to present the reactions when different medicines are mixed together to reduce the cost of pharmaceutical manufacturing. During surgeries, robots can automatically provide more accurate and fast operation on focus by controlling through computers.

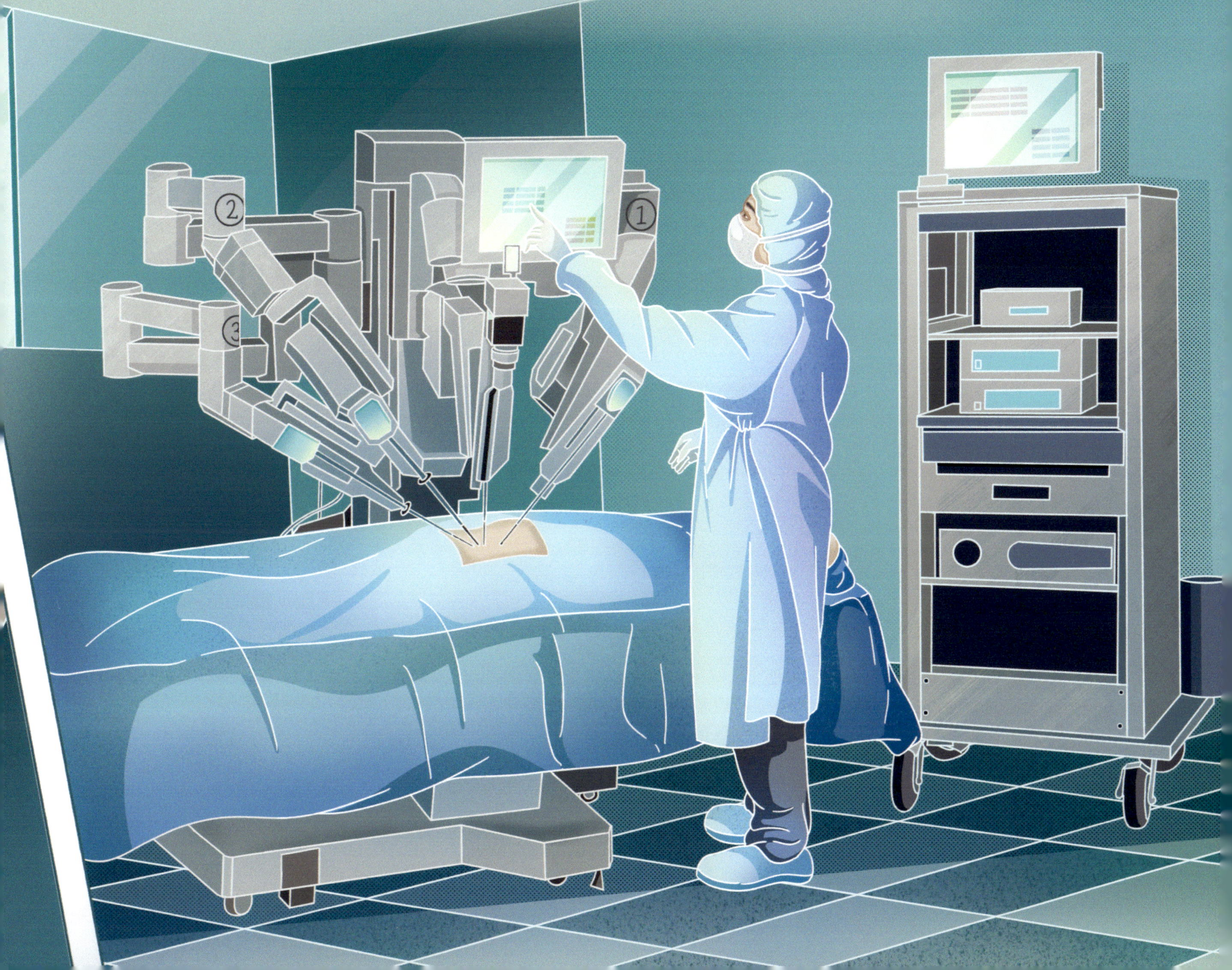

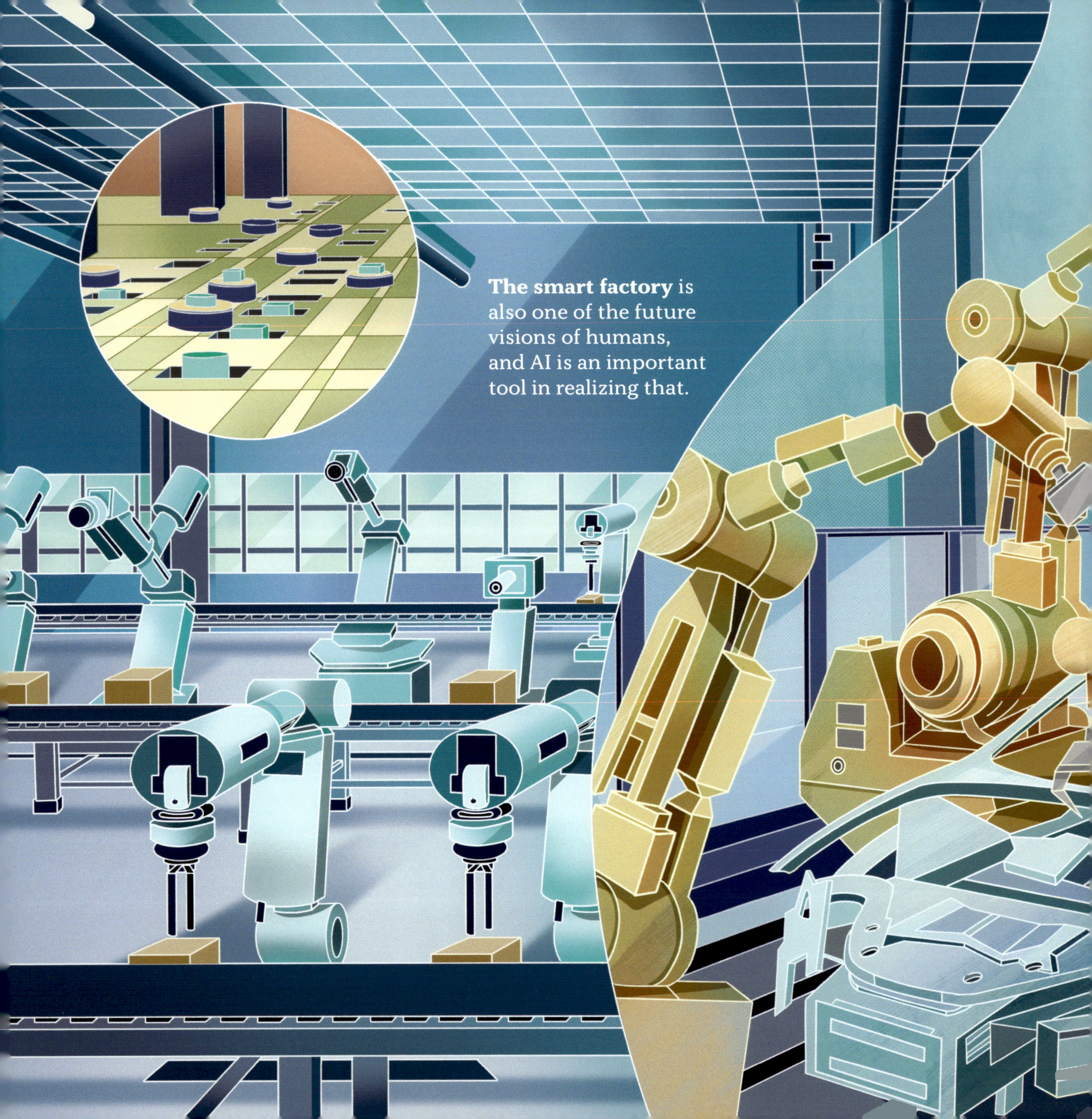

The smart factory is also one of the future visions of humans, and AI is an important tool in realizing that.

Nowadays, the number of factory workers has been decreasing with the deployment of robots.

Robots can transport data to the back end and conduct information analysis while operating. Once they identify device errors, the alarm will be triggered to remind workers to perform maintenance on time. On top of that, AI can even forecast the malfunction of devices in advance and formulate examination and repair plans accordingly.

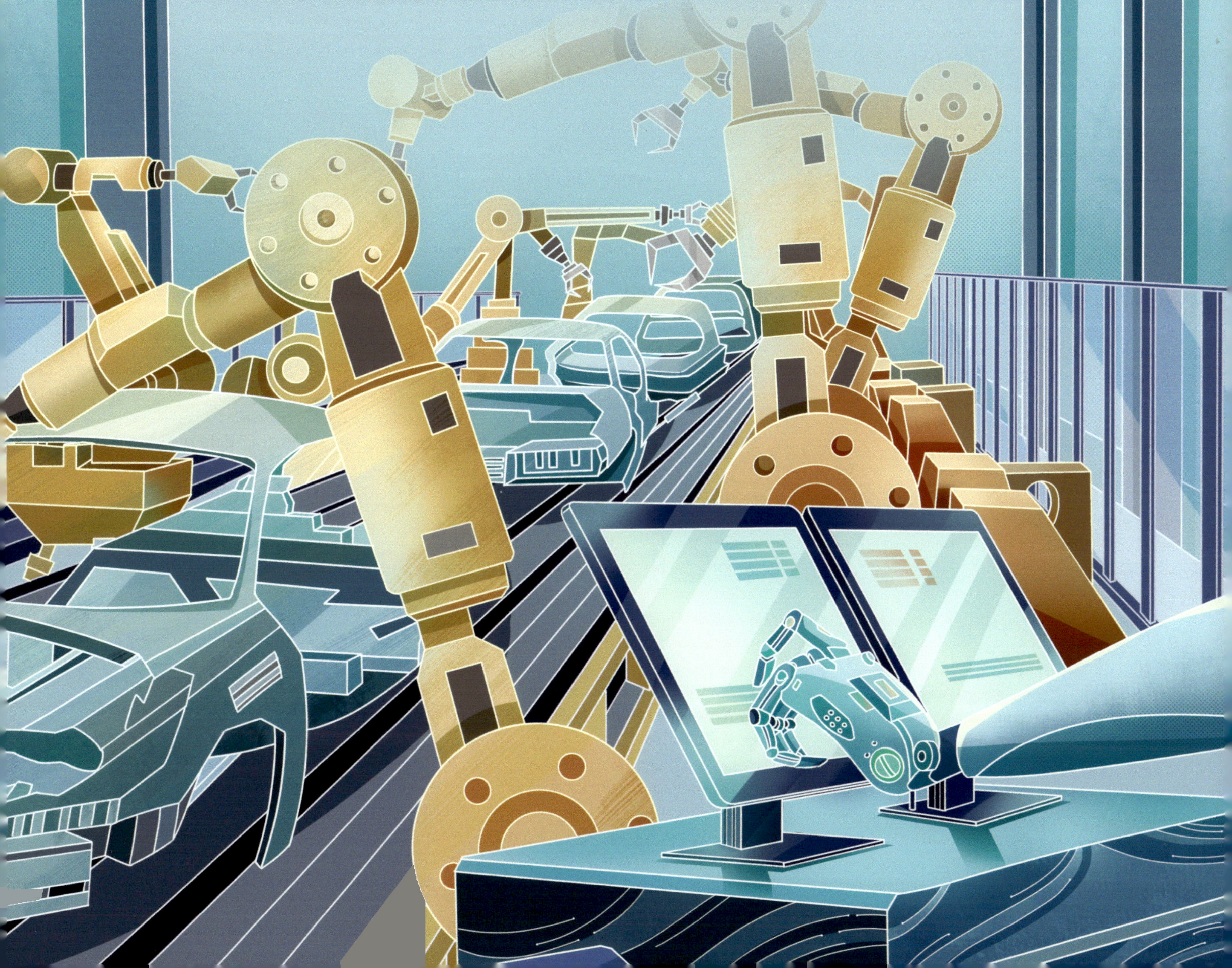

"Dongdong, let me ask you a tough question. Do you think schools should introduce AI?"

"Dad, let me think," Dongdong pondered for a while, "Yes, with AI, teachers don't need to grade papers themselves anymore."

In addition to **smart assessment**, people can now generate test questions using smart question banks, making creating exams easier. When encountering difficult problems, we can just take a photo, search for solutions, and learn by ourselves.

If we want to learn a new language, we can download software and speak with virtual characters to practice. We can also learn grammar and sentences by searching for translations.

AI not only played a significant role in the education sector but also performed impressively in the **financial industry.** Before investing in any company, we always have many questions regarding its financial performance, product quality, and customer scale. With an AI-backed investment advisor, it only takes seconds for us to receive a complete balance sheet that provides support for investment decision-making.

AI can also complete **financial forecasting for anti-fraud purposes** by summarizing and analyzing personal consumer behaviors, activities, and financial records to determine transaction authenticity and prevent risks.

“Dad, do we have AI at home then?” Dongdong asked.

“Of course! The smart speaker is one!”

Our phone can **remotely control** the robot vacuum to clean our rooms. When the weather gets warmer, it can turn on the AC and **automatically switches** it to the cooling mode.

We can find the TV program we'd like to watch through voice control.

We can also directly ask our TV for answers when we have questions.

The popular face-swapping video allows us to put one person's facial features on another person flawlessly, which even their family members couldn't recognize the difference. If we'd like to get a glimpse of our look 50 years from now, it only takes a click on the app and doesn't require putting on special makeup or changing clothes.

In addition, people have been researching how to allow visually impaired individuals to see the beautiful world through the eyes of the machines. Similarly, efforts have been made to enable non-verbal individuals to communicate by connecting machines with their brainwaves and produce speeches.

AI can help blind people to "see" the world.

AI can decipher brain waves.

Camera 1

Vehicle 100

Snapshot of Vehicles

Smart Navigation

In ancient times, transportation was inconvenient with only maps and compass available for use. People can barely reach their destinations without proper guidance. Now, with smart navigation systems, we can immediately have the most convenient routes and real-time traffic data offered to us by inputting our destination.

Automated vehicles

Automated vehicles can sense the traffic environment through the vehicle-mounted sensor system, then automatically plan its route and control the vehicles to arrive at planned destinations. Soon, everyone can commute by cars without actually driving it.

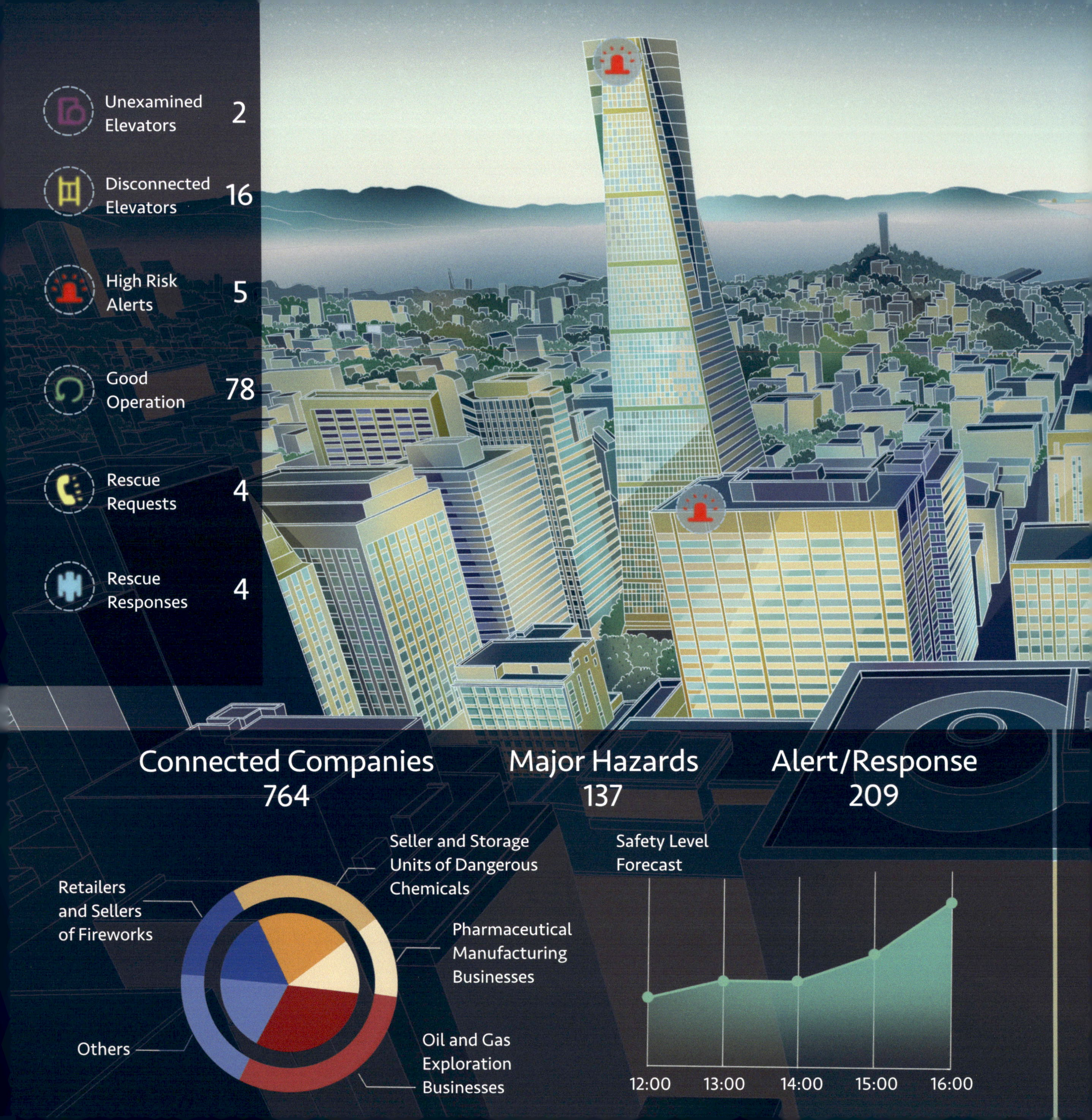
Unexamined Elevators 2
Disconnected Elevators 16
High Risk Alerts 5
Good Operation 78
Rescue Requests 4
Rescue Responses 4
Connected Companies 764
Major Hazards 137
Alert/Response 209
Seller and Storage Units of Dangerous Chemicals
Retailers and Sellers of Fireworks
Pharmaceutical Manufacturing Businesses
Others
Oil and Gas Exploration Businesses
Safety Level Forecast
12:00
13:00
14:00
15:00
16:00

What about the information exchange between each device? That falls into the research area of **Internet of Things (IoT)**, such as completing purchases in unguarded convenience stores and vendor machines.

The rapid development of IoT benefited from AI technology. It also helped build **smart factories, communities,** and even **earth** by combining it with AI and other technologies.

Trending Keywords

Stream Pollution

Illegal Production and Operation

Report Hazards to Police

Illegal Storage of Dangerous Items

Illegal Storage of Dangerous Chemicals

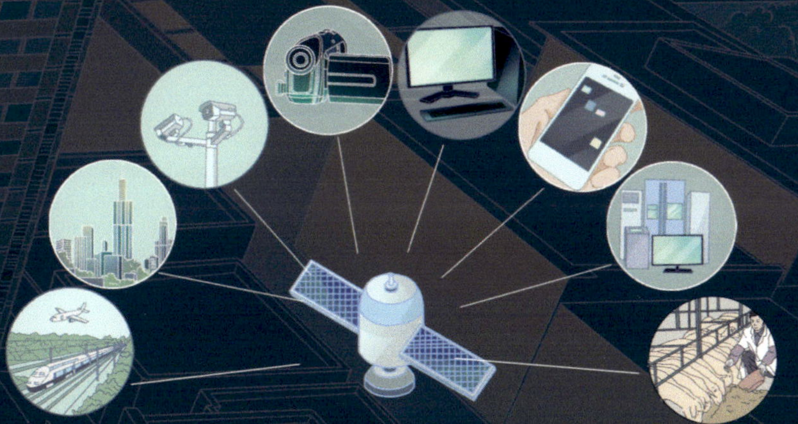

At present, the AI development in China is in the top-tier position around the world, especially in areas such as **voice recognition, facial recognition, machine translation, and Chinese information processing.**

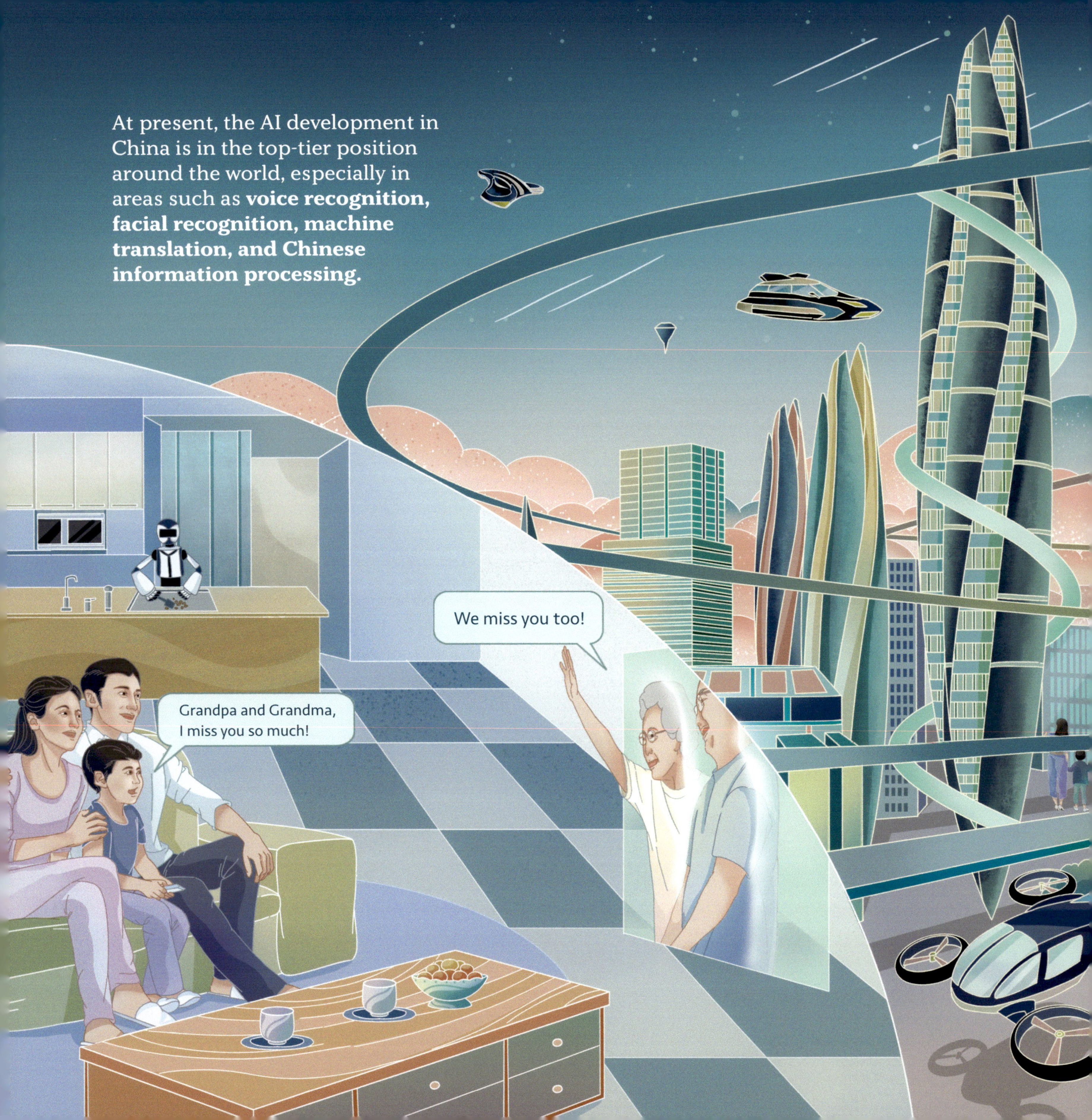

"Dad, will AI replace us one day if it's this powerful?" Dongdong starts to worry.

"AI is just a tool invented by humans. It hasn't reached the level of sophistication of human brains so far. Humans, as tool users, will always invent new tools to replace the ineffective ones."

The reason why humanity has been able to survive the countless disasters and catastrophes in human history is due to their quality of **collaboration and unity**. Humans have integrated such power into their belief, making it the civilization that passed down through generations. This is the enduring wellspring of human spirits.

Chinese Modern New Technology Series
Artificial Intelligence

Edited by Li Chaodong
Translated by Xuemeng Angela Li

First published in 2023 by Royal Collins Publishing Group Inc.
Groupe Publication Royal Collins Inc.
550-555 boul. René-Lévesque O Montréal (Québec) H2Z1B1 Canada

ISBN: 978-1-4878-1237-9

To find out more about our publications, please visit www.royalcollins.com.